LIVING WITH
ASTHMA

Peta Bee

RSVP
RAINTREE
STECK-VAUGHN
P U B L I S H E R S
A Steck-Vaughn Company

Austin, Texas

Titles in the series
Living with Asthma
Living with Diabetes
Living with Down Syndrome
Living with Epilepsy

Published by Raintree Steck-Vaughn Publishers,
an imprint of Steck-Vaughn Company

Library of Congress Cataloging-in-Publication Data
Bee, Peta.
Living with asthma / Peta Bee.
     p.   cm.—(Living with)
     Includes bibliographical references and index.
     Summary: Discusses the causes, nature, and symptoms
     of asthma, how it is affected by medicine, exercise, pets,
     and air quality, and what to do in an emergency.
     ISBN 0-8172-5568-0
     1. Asthma in children—Juvenile literature.
     [1. Asthma. 2. Diseases.]
     I. Title.
     RJ436.A68B44 2000
     618.92'238—dc21   98-18852

Printed in Italy. Bound in the United States.
1 2 3 4 5 6 7 8 9 0 03 02 01 00 99

Picture acknowledgments
The publishers would like to thank Ace cover (top), (Auschrombs) 28; Eye Ubiquitous
(Paul Thompson) 7, (David Cumming) 24; Getty Images (Andrew Syred) 8; Robert
Harding cover (middle), (Dr Muller) 20; James Davies Travel Photography 16; National
Asthma Campaign 29; Skjold 19; Wayland (Jeff Greenberg) 14, (Howard Davies) 15
(below). All the other photographs were taken for this book by Angela Hampton. Most of
the people who are photographed in this book are models.

While every effort has been made to secure permission, in one case it has proved
impossible to trace the copyright holder.

The illustration on page 6 is by Michael Courtney.

Contents

Meet Rachel, John, and Nicola

Rachel, John, and Nicola are children like you. They are about your age and go to schools like yours. After school and on weekends they are all very busy doing things that they enjoy.

Rachel is a very good swimmer. She belongs to a swimming club and swims in her local pool twice a week. Her favorite stroke is the backstroke. She hopes that one day she will win a gold medal swimming in the Olympic Games.

△ Rachel works hard at her swimming. She is one of the fastest swimmers in her school.

◁ John's ambition is to play soccer for his country.

▽ Nicola and her friends spend hours practicing dance routines.

Nicola loves being with her best friends. They enjoy listening to music and dancing.

Rachel, John, and Nicola all lead very different lives. But they have one thing in common. Each of them has a condition called asthma. Millions of people have asthma, so the young people are not alone. Asthma is serious because it can make breathing difficult, but it doesn't mean you have to stop enjoying yourself. Rachel, John, and Nicola have learned to take control of their asthma so that they can enjoy all their favorite activities.

John prefers to play soccer and take part in other sports. He is on the school soccer team and practices his soccer skills every day when he gets home. He is also a very fast runner and finished first in a race at his school last summer.

What Is Asthma?

Asthma is due to an allergic reaction in the lungs. It is a condition that affects the airways—the small tubes that allow air in and out of the lungs. People with asthma may feel short of breath so that they wheeze or cough. Sometimes coughing can leave their chests feeling tight and uncomfortable.

When people have asthma, their airways are sensitive. If they come into contact with something called an asthma trigger, their airways may become inflamed. This can happen if they catch a cold or if they breathe in other allergens (things that they are allergic to).

An asthma trigger is something that makes asthma worse. Some of the most common asthma triggers are colds or other virus infections.

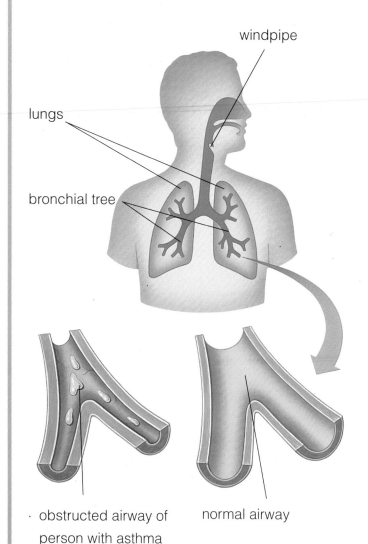

windpipe

lungs

bronchial tree

obstructed airway of person with asthma

normal airway

◁ This diagram shows how the airways are affected by asthma.

John's asthma is made worse by house dust mites and cat dander. His grandmother has a cat named Jessie, so John has to take medicine before he visits her. Nicola's asthma is triggered by traffic fumes and poor air quality. Grass pollen, poor air quality, and exercise make Rachel's asthma worse.

△ Traffic fumes make some people's asthma worse.

If you have asthma, it is important to know what things trigger your asthma so that you can try to avoid them.

If people who have asthma come into contact with their asthma triggers, they find it hard to breathe. It can be quite frightening when this happens. But special asthma medicines can help them breathe normally.

What Is a House Dust Mite?

House dust mites are triggers for many people with asthma. They are tiny (about 30 fit on the head of a pin), so you can't see them without a microscope. But there could be as many as 2 million of them living in your mattress!

The mites live in dust that builds up around the house. They live just about everywhere—in carpets, curtains, bedclothes, and soft furniture, such as sofas and armchairs.

△ A house dust mite, about 1,000 times bigger than its real size.

The main cause of allergies for people with asthma is the droppings left behind by mites. Although the droppings are tiny, they float in the air with the dust, so it is easy to breathe them in. If people with asthma breathe in the droppings, they can irritate their airways and trigger asthma.

There are lots of things you can do to reduce the number of house dust mites in your home. Make sure your room is dusted regularly with a damp cloth, and put all your clothes away. Piles of clothes on the floor make the perfect home for house dust mites. Open the bedroom window in the morning, too. House dust mites don't like cold air.

◁ Dusting with a damp cloth regularly helps keep down the dust in the bedroom.

How Asthma Medicine Can Help

There are lots of medicines that make it easier for people with asthma to live normal lives. Before giving out medicine, the doctor may measure your breathing with something called a peak flow meter and will ask about your symptoms. Then, the doctor or the nurse will give you some asthma medicine to breathe in, usually using devices called inhalers.

Rachel's doctor gave her two special inhalers that help her breathe more easily. One is called a reliever and the other is called a preventer. Both medicines contain drugs that help control her asthma.

△ The doctor is showing Rachel the reliever inhaler.

▷ Rachel is learning how to use her preventer inhaler.

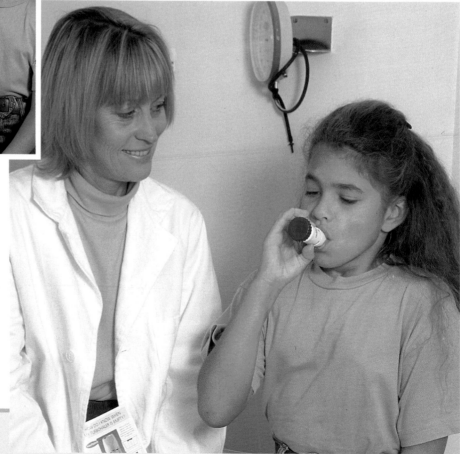

▷ Rachel uses her reliever inhaler when she feels her breathing is becoming worse.

Rachel's reliever inhaler

"My reliever inhaler is blue. I use it when I first feel my asthma coming on. It makes the muscles in my airways relax so I can breathe easily again. I can't always tell when I might get asthma symptoms, so I always carry my reliever inhaler with me."

Rachel has a brown preventer inhaler that helps calm down her airways. She uses it first thing in the morning and last thing at night, even when she is well. Not all preventer inhalers are brown; some are white, orange, or red. Many preventer inhalers contain a low dose of steroids. Using a preventer inhaler means that Rachel is less likely to have an asthma attack if she comes into contact with her asthma triggers. This is one way for her to keep her asthma under control.

Avoiding Asthma Triggers at Home

If people with asthma come into contact with their triggers all the time, they are likely to have asthma symptoms more often. John's mother, Gina, is careful to help John avoid his asthma triggers around their home. She can do many things to protect him.

John has special covers for his mattress, comforter, and pillow. These are made of a material that keeps the dust mites inside so that he can't breathe in the droppings when he is asleep. Gina washes John's bedclothes at a hot temperature every week to get rid of mite droppings. She also vacuums his bedroom often.

Gina opens the windows every day to let in plenty of fresh air. House dust mites don't like cold, fresh air! She also dusts the furniture with a damp cloth to remove any mites.

▽ It is a good idea to vacuum every day, using a good vacuum cleaner that does not spread the dust around.

▷ To reduce condensation, Gina makes sure the kitchen window is open when John helps her cook.

House dust mites love warm, damp air. John is sensitive to cold, dry air as well as many cooking odors. John's mother always keeps the kitchen door closed when she is cooking to keep the odors from spreading to other parts of the house.

When Rachel plays outside, she tries to avoid things that will make her asthma worse. Grass pollen is the main problem, but the pollen in flowers can also trigger her asthma. Rachel does not bring fresh flowers into the house.

◁ Rachel is allergic to grass pollen, but she can play outside if she is careful.

13

Exercise Is Good for You

Exercise is a great way to keep fit and have fun. Unfortunately, it is also one of the most common asthma triggers. Everyone gets out of breath when they exercise, but if you have asthma, you may wheeze and cough after the exercise has stopped. If this happens, you should tell your doctor or nurse the next time you visit.

◁ Keeping fit is just as important for people with asthma as for anyone else.

Having asthma doesn't mean you should stop exercising. In fact, regular exercise can actually help your asthma. The fitter you become, the better your lungs work and the fewer problems you should have with asthma.

Some sports are less likely to bring on asthma than others. Tennis and sprinting, where the exercise is in short bursts, tend not to trigger asthma.

▷ The warm, damp air in the pool helps relieve Rachel's airways.

Swimming is a good choice for some people with asthma. The air at pools is damp and warm, so it doesn't irritate their lungs.

Exercise is a trigger for Rachel's asthma, but she has learned to make sure that her swimming doesn't cause her to have an asthma attack.

Rachel uses her preventer inhaler every day. Before she exercises, she takes her reliever inhaler. Then, she warms up by doing some short sprints in the hallway before she goes into the swimming pool. This means that doing exercise isn't such a shock to her system.

◁ Having asthma doesn't mean you can't become successful at sports.

What About Pets?

Pets can be great fun. John loves animals, especially cats, and he would love to have a kitten of his own. But animals are a common trigger for asthma. When John comes into contact with pet fur or bird feathers, it makes his asthma worse.

If you have asthma, it is a good idea not to keep pets that have feathers or fur. But it is not only animal hair that can cause problems. Tiny flakes of animal skin can get into the air with dust and be breathed in by people with asthma. Even the urine of pets such as cats, dogs, guinea pigs, rabbits, and gerbils can cause problems for some people.

There are just a few pets such as stick insects and goldfish that may not cause problems. But that doesn't mean that people with asthma have to stay away from animals altogether.

▷ It is important to brush pets regularly to remove loose fur.

▷ If you have asthma, it is not a good idea to keep a cat as a pet. Even when the cat goes outside, the cat allergens can stay in the house for several hours.

The saliva left on a cat's fur after it has washed can also trigger asthma. To make sure John is protected, his grandmother always wipes her cat's fur with a damp cloth before John visits. Even so, the cat allergens can remain suspended in the air for hours. Avoidance is the best treatment if you are allergic to cats. For John, it is better if his grandmother visits him without her cat.

Going on Vacation

$\triangledown$ John collects all his asthma medicines to make sure he does not forget anything.

When John goes on vacation with his family, he makes advance plans, to make sure he enjoys it as much as everyone else.

Being away from home means lots of changes, and there are many things that can trigger asthma on vacation. There is no one destination that is the best place for people with asthma to go, because everyone's asthma is so different.

John is prepared

"Before I leave, I make sure I've packed enough of my asthma medicine to last the whole time. I pack spare inhalers just in case I lose one. Also, I take my preventer medicine before we actually go, as well as while we're away. That means I'm less likely to have problems while we're gone."

Weather conditions, pollen levels, and air pollution will vary wherever you go. Some people with asthma find that certain weather conditions make their asthma worse. If John and his family go overseas, they will choose a place where the weather is warm, but not very hot. Dry, hot places can be dusty. The dust might irritate John's airways. John's older brother, Steven, keeps an eye on the local weather changes when they are on vacation.

Poor Air Quality

Unfortunately, the air we inhale is not always clean and fresh. The quality of air is often poor and contains lots of different things that can make asthma worse. Outdoor air contains natural triggers such as pollen and ground-level ozone.

◁ It is hard to avoid traffic fumes. Breathing in outdoor air can trigger asthma.

Air also contains unnatural pollutants. Car exhaust fumes release gases and small particles into the air. There are other pollutants, such as cigarette smoke. Sometimes the levels of these pollutants can irritate the lungs of people with asthma.

△ Breathing through a scarf can warm the air you take into your lungs.

Nicola protects herself

"When it's really cold, I wrap a scarf over my nose and mouth when I'm walking to school. It keeps out the cold air. I find I wheeze and cough less then."

Every day Nicola's family listens to a forecast for air pollution levels. The forecast will say if there will be high levels of certain gases, such as nitrogen dioxide and ozone, in the air that day. Ozone is a potent cause of asthma.

If poor air quality triggers your asthma, it is better not to do too much exercise outdoors on very hot summer afternoons, when ground-level ozone levels are at their highest.

21

What to Do in an Emergency

E mma is Rachel's best friend. She doesn't have asthma, but she knows what to do if Rachel has an asthma attack when she is around. Emma and Rachel know that asthma can be very dangerous, so they both make sure they are prepared in case of emergency.

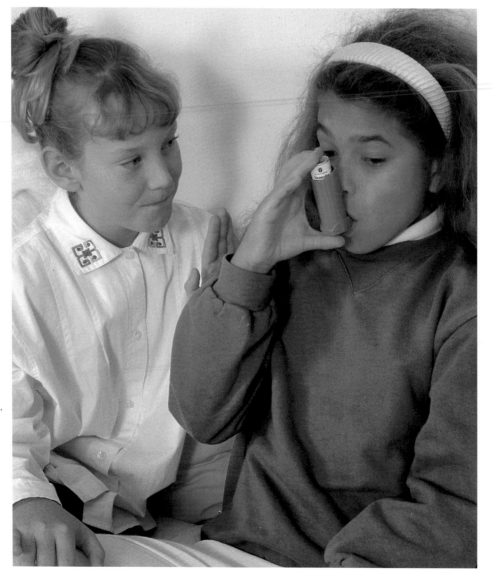

◁ Rachel has learned exactly what to do in an emergency and how to use her inhaler correctly. Emma has also learned all about Rachel's different medicines.

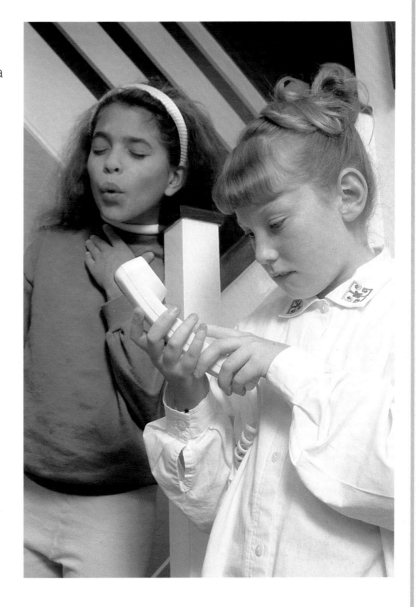

▷ Emma's dad has called for an ambulance. Now Emma is calling Rachel's mother to tell her that Rachel is not well.

First, Emma tries to keep Rachel calm by talking to her. Although this is not easy when Rachel is finding it hard to breathe, Emma knows that panicking will only make things worse. Then, she gets Rachel to sit up straight and tells her to breathe slowly and calmly.

Emma knows that Rachel always keeps her reliever inhaler in her school bag, so she gets it and Rachel takes two puffs immediately. If Rachel is still not feeling better after a few minutes, Emma will go for an adult, who may need to call for an ambulance. Rachel will keep taking her inhaler every five to ten minutes until medical help arrives.

If Emma isn't around when she has an asthma attack, Rachel knows that she needs to tell an adult to get medical help quickly, especially if she thinks her inhaler isn't working properly.

How Would You Manage?

Have you ever wondered what it's like to have asthma? Remember, like Rachel, Nicola, and John, if you have asthma, you have it all the time. Your airways are always sensitive, although you only have asthma symptoms when you come into contact with one of your triggers or forget to take your medicine.

Asthma will be present all day every day, and it can affect everything you do. We have seen that there are lots of things that can be done to help people with asthma so they can lead normal lives.

△ Everyone needs exercise to keep fit. If they take care, people with asthma can enjoy sports like everybody else.

▷ People with asthma are no different from anyone else, but sometimes they have to make changes to their lives.

Think about the sorts of problems that people with asthma might face every day. Write down what you would do to reduce these problems if you had asthma.

Think about the different things that trigger asthma when you are away from home. What kinds of things could you do to lessen asthma triggers in cold weather? What would you do before you play sports?

Write down what you would do to avoid three different asthma triggers such as poor air quality, house dust mites, and pollen from weeds or grasses.

Making Life Easier

△ John's spacer device helps his asthma medicine work quickly.

Life can be made easier in many ways for people with asthma. Children like John, Nicola, and Rachel take different kinds of medicines to help them control their asthma.

Not all asthma medicines are suitable for everyone, so doctors and nurses help people with asthma decide which ones are best for them. There are tablets and a variety of inhalers that contain mild steroids. These are medicines that help make the airways less swollen. Taken regularly, these medicines will help control asthma.

There are other ways to make life easier, too. John uses a spacer device to take his preventer treatment every morning and evening. This can help the medicine reach his airways, where it is needed most.

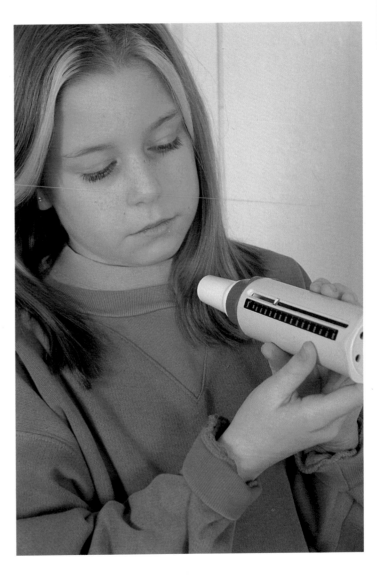

▽ A peak flow meter shows Nicola how well she is breathing.

Nicola checks her peak flow regularly to keep track of how good or bad her asthma is at any time. Peak flow meters measure how hard you can blow out. When Nicola's asthma is under control, she can blow out a lot of air, and her peak flow reading is higher. Nicola also monitors her asthma symptoms.

Sometimes Rachel's asthma is really bad, and she finds it hard to control her symptoms. Then, Rachel's doctor prescribes some steroid tablets for her. These contain a higher dose of medicine. She takes them for just a few days until her asthma is back under control.

Rachel, John, and Nicola have all learned to take important steps to control their asthma.

Getting Help

There are many places where you can get advice, information, and support about living with asthma.

Your doctor and asthma nurse will be able to give you advice on the type of asthma medicine that is best for you. They are there to help you. Always talk to them if you are worried about anything linked to asthma.

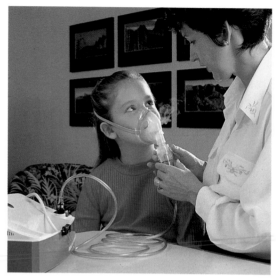

Most doctors' offices and hospital community outreach programs will provide a great deal of free information, including pamphlets and brochures, about asthma. These may be geared to young asthmatics and will include a variety of ways of describing how to deal with asthma.

△ Talking to an asthma nurse will provide answers to the questions you may have about your asthma.

In addition, several organizations sponsor Internet links that provide current information for people who want to know more about asthma and how to treat it.

American Academy of Allegy, Asthma, and Immunology
611 E. Wells Street
Milwaukee, WI 53202
1-800-822-2762
http://www.aaaai.org

American College of Allergy, Asthma, and Immunology
85 W. Algonquin Rd., Suite 550
Arlington Heights, IL 60005
1-847-427-1200
http://www.allergy.mcg.edu

Local newspapers and radio and TV stations provide air quality forecasts.

Allernet
A worldwide source of allegy and asthma public education located on the internet at http://www.allernet.com

Food Allegy Network—http://www.foodallergy.org
This is a nonprofit organization funded in part by Kraft Foods. It has useful information for food allergy patients.

There are also regional groups where people meet to discuss issues surrounding asthma. You and your parents or carers are welcome to go along to the local meetings in your area.

Glossary

Allergen Anything that causes an allergic reaction, often particular foods, pollen, fur, or dust.

Asthma trigger Something that causes asthma symptoms to become worse.

Condensation When water vapor turns to water, often on a window.

Ground-level ozone Bright sunlight makes a chemical reaction in the air, which produces ozone at ground level. This ground-level ozone can inflame the airways of people with asthma.

Inflammation When a part of the body is inflamed, it becomes hot, red, and sore.

Inhaler A device for breathing medicine into the lungs, through the mouth.

Peak flow The measurement of how much air you can blow out.

Pollutants Substances that damage the environment. Small particles of pollutants in the air can make breathing difficult and trigger asthma in some people.

Preventer inhaler A device that contains drugs that calm down the airways so that an asthma attack is less likely to happen.

Reliever inhaler A device that contains drugs that relax the muscles in the airways so that it is easier to breathe.

Spacer A device that is used with an inhaler to help a person breathe in more medication.

Steroids Drugs that make the airways less swollen.

Symptom A change in a person's health that can show that he or she has a disease. A symptom is something you feel or see, like a pain or rash.

Further Information

BOOKS

Adams, Francis V. *The Asthma Sourcebook: Everything You Need to Know*. Los Angeles: Lowell House, 1996.

American Lung Advisory Group. *The American Lung Association Family Guide to Asthma and Allergies: How You and Your Children Can Breathe Easier*. Boston: Little Brown, 1998.

Hyde, Margaret O. *Living With Asthma*. New York: Walker and Co., 1995.

Polk, Irwin J. *All About Asthma: Stop Suffering and Start Living*. New York: Plenum, 1997.

Silverstein, Alvin. *Asthma* (Diseases and People). Springfield, NJ: Enslow Publishing, 1997.

ADDRESSES

The American Academy of Allergy and Immunology
611 East Wells Street
Milwaukee, WI 53202

American Medical Association
535 North Dearborn Street
Chicago, IL 60610

National Institutes of Health
9000 Rockville Pike
Bethseda, MD 20892

U.S. Public Health Service
5600 Fishers Lane
Bethseda, MD 20857

Index

Numbers in **bold** show subjects shown in pictures.